COUNTRY PROFILES

CANADA

BY EMILY ROSE OACHS

BELLWETHER MEDIA • MINNEAPOLIS, MN

Blastoff! Discovery launches a new mission: reading to learn. Filled with facts and features, each book offers you an exciting new world to explore!

This edition first published in 2018 by Bellwether Media, Inc.

No part of this publication may be reproduced in whole or in part without written permission of the publisher.
For information regarding permission, write to Bellwether Media, Inc., Attention: Permissions Department,
5357 Penn Avenue South, Minneapolis, MN 55419.

Library of Congress Cataloging-in-Publication Data

Names: Oachs, Emily Rose, author.
Title: Canada / by Emily Rose Oachs.
Description: Minneapolis, MN : Bellwether Media, Inc., 2018.
| Series: Blastoff! Discovery: Country Profiles | Includes
bibliographical references and index. | Audience: Grades 3-8.
| Audience: Ages 7-13.
Identifiers: LCCN 2016053597 (print)|
  LCCN 2016055179 (ebook) | ISBN 9781626176775
  (hardcover : alkaline paper) | ISBN 9781681034072
  (ebook)
Subjects: LCSH: Canada–Juvenile literature.
Classification: LCC F1008.2 .O23 2018 (print) | LCC F1008.2
  (ebook) | DDC971–dc23
LC record available at https://lccn.loc.gov/2016053597

Editor: Christina Leaf   Designer: Jon Eppard

Printed in the United States of America, North Mankato, MN.

TABLE OF CONTENTS

BANFF NATIONAL PARK

Two hikers hit the trail in Canada's Banff National Park. They are among the millions of visitors that flock to this popular **landmark** each year. As they hike, the snow-capped Canadian Rockies tower above them. The peaks seem to pierce the bright blue sky.

OTHER TOP SITES

CHÂTEAU FRONTENAC

CN TOWER

NIAGARA FALLS

TOTEM POLES IN GWAII HAANAS NATIONAL PARK

MORAINE LAKE
BANFF NATIONAL PARK

The trail leads the hikers high into the mountains. Forests cover the valleys and hills below them. In the distance, the hikers spot a vast, white glacier on a mountaintop. After a few miles, they come upon a smooth, turquoise lake that reflects the mountains around them. This is Canada!

5

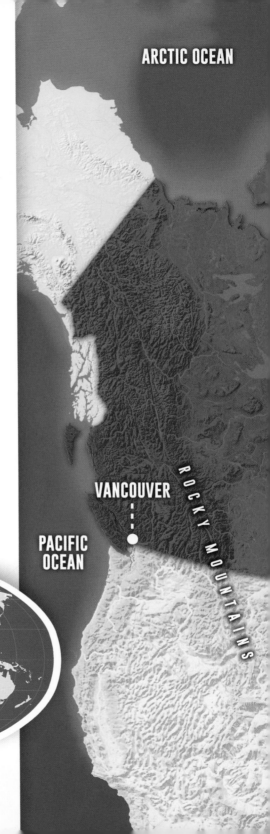

ARCTIC OCEAN

ROCKY MOUNTAINS

VANCOUVER

PACIFIC OCEAN

LOCATION

Canada stretches across 3,855,103 square miles (9,984,670 square kilometers) of northern North America. The country's capital is Ottawa. It is located in the southeast. Canada shares its southern and western borders with the United States. Four **Great Lakes** make up part of the southern boundary.

Three oceans touch Canada. The Atlantic Ocean sits to the east, while the Pacific Ocean lies to the west. In the north is the Arctic Ocean. Many Canadian islands rise from this ocean's icy waters.

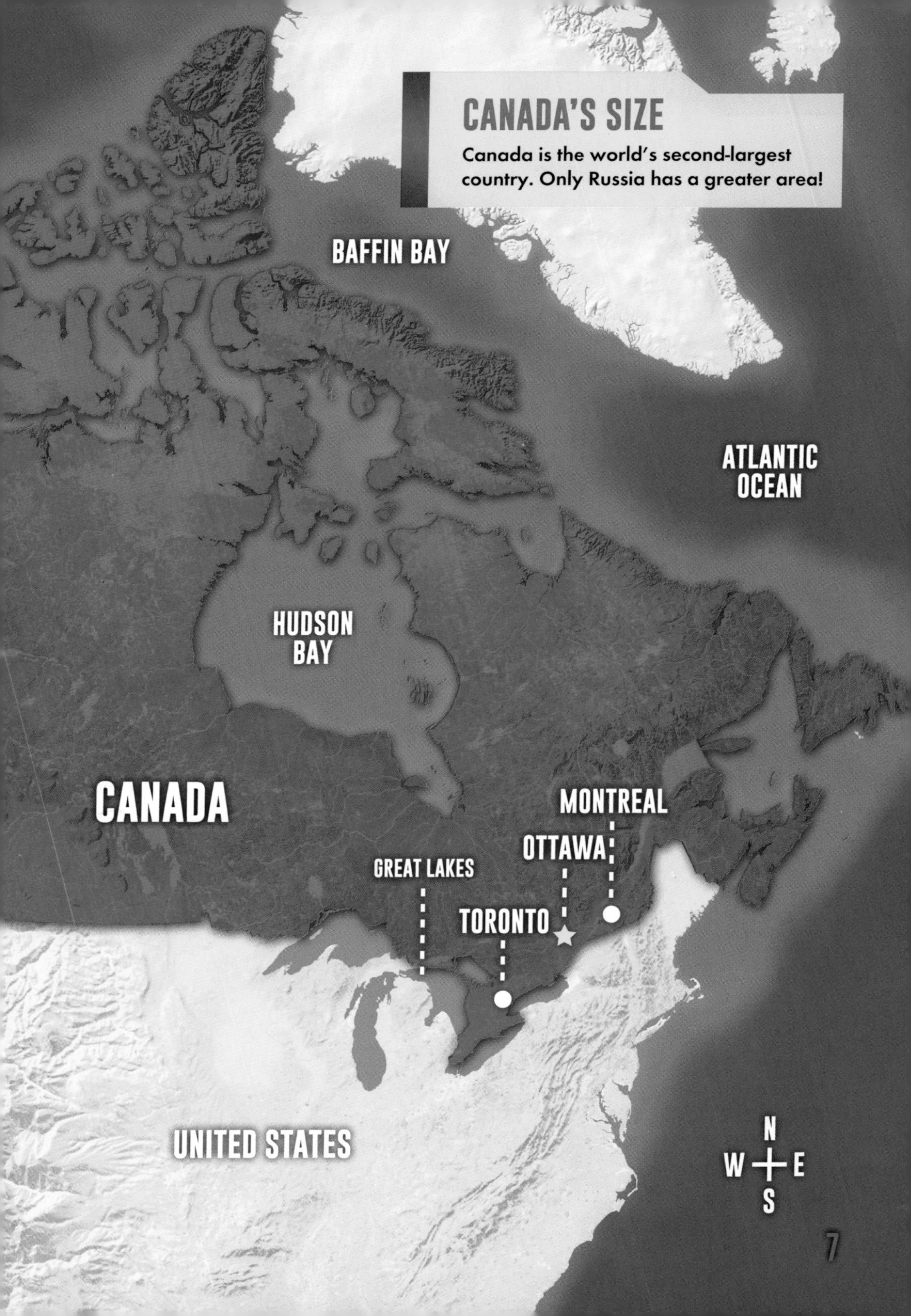

BAFFIN BAY
ATLANTIC OCEAN
HUDSON BAY
CANADA
MONTREAL
OTTAWA
GREAT LAKES
TORONTO
UNITED STATES
N
W
E
S

CANADA'S SIZE

Canada is the world's second-largest country. Only Russia has a greater area!

LANDSCAPE AND CLIMATE

Tall mountain ranges rise along Canada's western coast. Just east of these ranges stand the Rocky Mountains. Dense forests blanket their slopes. Beyond the Rockies sits a belt of grassy lowlands called the Interior **Plains**. A U-shaped area called the Canadian Shield stretches across most of eastern Canada. Forests, rolling hills, and thousands of lakes are found there. Northern Canada's islands lie in the Arctic. There, the land is cold, dry **tundra**.

= CANADIAN SHIELD

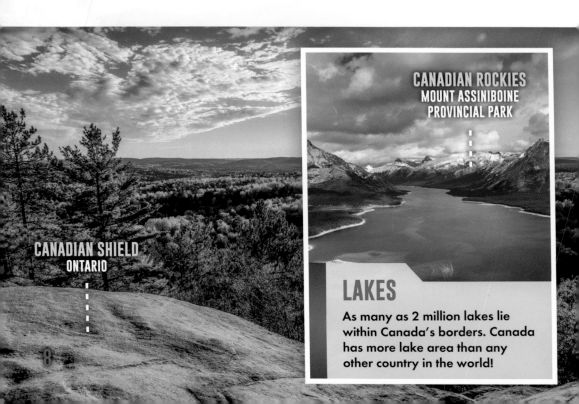

CANADIAN SHIELD
ONTARIO

CANADIAN ROCKIES
MOUNT ASSINIBOINE
PROVINCIAL PARK

LAKES

As many as 2 million lakes lie within Canada's borders. Canada has more lake area than any other country in the world!

TUNDRA
TOMBSTONE TERRITORIAL
PARK, YUKON

OTTAWA

Average seasonal highs and lows

JANUARY
HIGH: 19 °F (-7 °C)
LOW: 0 °F (-18 °C)

APRIL
HIGH: 52 °F (11 °C)
LOW: 28 °F (-2 °C)

JULY
HIGH: 79 °F (26 °C)
LOW: 54 °F (12 °C)

OCTOBER
HIGH: 55 °F (13 °C)
LOW: 36 °F (2 °C)

°F = degrees Fahrenheit
°C = degrees Celsius

Most of Canada sees very cold winters. Only the western coast has mild, wet weather. Southern summers can be hot and humid. In the Arctic, summers are short and cool.

WILDLIFE

Canada's national **symbol** is the beaver. This animal makes its home along Canada's lakes and rivers. In the icy Arctic, foxes and wolves feed on lemmings. Polar bears hunt seals along northern coasts. Each summer, Canada geese **migrate** to the tundra to nest.

Forests are home to moose and caribou. Furry Canada lynxes stalk snowshoe hares between the trees. Mountain goats and bighorn sheep roam the western mountains. Pronghorn bound across Canada's grasslands. Snowy owls are common around the country.

BEAVER

SNOWY OWL

CARIBOU

BIGHORN SHEEP

- - - CANADA LYNX

10

THE LOONIE

Canada's one-dollar coin features the image of a loon on one side. This earned the coin the nickname "loonie."

POLAR BEAR - - - - -

POLAR BEAR

Life Span: **25 to 30 years**
Red List Status: **vulnerable**

polar bear range = ■

LEAST CONCERN	NEAR THREATENED	VULNERABLE	ENDANGERED	CRITICALLY ENDANGERED	EXTINCT IN THE WILD	EXTINCT
		▲				

Canada's name probably comes from the word *kanata*. This Huron-Iroquois word means "village" or "settlement." Other suggested names for Canada included Borealia, Efisga, and Tuponia.

More than 35 million people live in Canada. Most Canadians have **ancestors** from Europe. Small populations of **First Nations** and Inuit people also call Canada home. Their ancestors lived in Canada before the first Europeans arrived. *Métis* Canadians count **native** peoples and early fur traders among their ancestors. Canada also welcomes many **immigrants** from countries around the world.

Most Canadians practice Christianity. In cities, Islam, Hinduism, and Sikhism are becoming more common as immigrants settle there. Many Canadians do not follow any religion. English and French are Canada's two official languages, though English is more common.

FAMOUS FACE

Name: Wayne Gretzky
Birthday: January 26, 1961
Hometown: Brantford, Ontario, Canada
Famous for: Record-breaking professional hockey player in the National Hockey League (NHL) who was named Most Valuable Player nine times

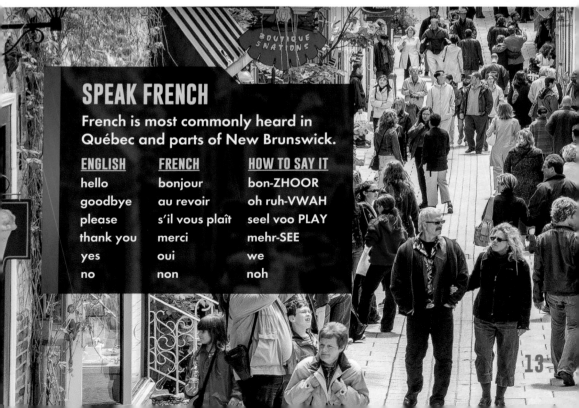

SPEAK FRENCH

French is most commonly heard in Québec and parts of New Brunswick.

ENGLISH	FRENCH	HOW TO SAY IT
hello	bonjour	bon-ZHOOR
goodbye	au revoir	oh ruh-VWAH
please	s'il vous plaît	seel voo PLAY
thank you	merci	mehr-SEE
yes	oui	we
no	non	noh

COMMUNITIES

Most Canadians make their homes in and around cities near the southern border, such as Toronto and Vancouver. Families tend to live with just their small **nuclear families** in **urban** apartments or houses just outside the city.

TORONTO

In the countryside, Canadians usually have larger homes and families. Some work close to home. Others use the nation's freeways to travel into cities to work each day. About half of First Nations people live on **reserves**. Their families and communities tend to be large and tight-knit.

Canadians are known for being polite. In the east, Canadians are also considered reserved and old-fashioned. In the west, they are more relaxed and modern. Many French customs are common in the **province** of Québec. There, French speakers may greet friends with a kiss on the cheek. While speaking, they often gesture more broadly than English speakers do.

Many native peoples carry on the **traditions** of their ancestors. They still hunt, trap, dance, drum, and carve as their ancestors did.

Each province controls its own education system in Canada. Young Canadians must enter school at age 5 or 6. Public schools are free through secondary school. After that, students often go on to attend universities or community colleges. Low costs allow many Canadians to continue their education.

Most Canadians have **service jobs**. They may work for the government, or in hospitals, schools, or restaurants. Lumber, fish, oil, and natural gas are major **natural resources**. Canadian workers process and **export** these materials. Other important exports include machinery and wheat.

DOCTOR

OIL WORKERS

ICE HOCKEY

Canada boasts two national sports, ice hockey and lacrosse. The country is proud of its connection to hockey. When not playing in their own games, children and adults alike love to cheer on their favorite teams. Wayne Gretzky, Gordie Howe, and many other hockey greats hail from Canada.

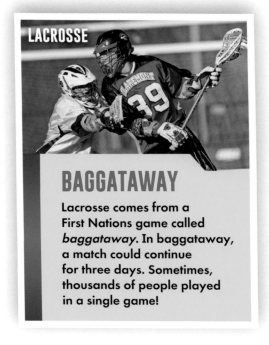

LACROSSE

BAGGATAWAY

Lacrosse comes from a First Nations game called *baggataway*. In baggataway, a match could continue for three days. Sometimes, thousands of people played in a single game!

Skiing, ice skating, and curling are other favorite winter sports. In the summer, lacrosse takes over. The country's vast national parks also give Canadians the chance to fish, hike, camp, and canoe.

CURLING

INDOOR CURLING

What You Need:
- 6 colored beanbags (3 in one color, 3 in a different color)
- roll of masking tape
- smooth, uncarpeted floor

How to Play:
1. Use the masking tape to outline a target on the floor. It should have three rings.
2. Mark a tape line on the floor at least 10 feet (3 meters) from the target. Players must release their beanbags before reaching this line.
3. Players take turns sliding beanbags toward the target. Bags should be like curling stones, slid by a player lunging forward. A player can use beanbags to bump opposing bags out of the way.
4. After all beanbags have been thrown, whoever threw the beanbag closest to the bullseye wins the round. That player earns one point for each beanbag that is closer than their opponent's.
5. Play at least two rounds. The player who scored on the previous round throws first the next round. Whoever has the most points at the end of the game wins!

In Canada, people eat breakfast before work or school. Families often gather for dinner around six in the evening. It is the biggest meal of the day. During meals, Canadians generally keep their forks in their left hands while both cutting and eating.

Poutine is among Canada's most popular foods. The dish features a pile of French fries topped with gravy and cheese curds. On Christmas, a meat-filled pie called *tourtière* is common. It can be made with pork, beef, salmon, or other meats. For breakfast, Canadians may drizzle their country's famous maple syrup over their pancakes or crêpes.

POUTINE

TOURTIÈRE

MAPLE SYRUP TAFFY RECIPE

Ingredients:
1 cup maple syrup
snow

Steps:

1. Collect fresh, clean snow into a cake pan.

2. With an adult present, pour maple syrup into a saucepan. Bring the maple syrup to a boil.

3. Boil the maple syrup until it reaches 235 degrees Fahrenheit (113 degrees Celsius). Then take the saucepan off the heat.

4. Immediately pour the hot maple syrup over the snow. Wait a few minutes for the maple syrup to cool, then grab it and eat!

LOTS OF SYRUP

More maple syrup comes from Canada than from anywhere else in the world. In 2014, the country produced more than 9 million gallons (34 million liters)!

**CANADA DAY
CELEBRATION**

June and July hold many important Canadian holidays. On June 21, Canadians celebrate the history of their country's native people for National **Aboriginals** Day. Saint-Jean-Baptiste Day on June 24 honors the **patron saint** of Canada's French speakers. Bonfires and parades mark this national holiday for Québec.

   Each year, Canada Day salutes the nation's founding
on July 1. Canadians watch dazzling fireworks displays
and dress in red and white to celebrate their nation's birth.
October brings Thanksgiving feasts of turkey, sweet potatoes,
and pumpkin pie. Canadians across the country use this
holiday to reflect on all that they are thankful for.

AROUND 1000 CE
Shores of modern-day Newfoundland settled by Vikings

1600s
Fur trade boom begins

1534
Land along Saint Lawrence River claimed by French explorers and named New France

1949

Admittance of
Newfoundland and
Labrador to Canada
as its tenth and
final province

2015

Justin Trudeau
is elected
prime minister

1867

Dominion of Canada
formed from the provinces
of New Brunswick, Quebec,
Nova Scotia, and Ontario

1897

Start of the Klondike
Gold Rush in the
Yukon Territory

1763

The Treaty of Paris
places New France
under the control
of Britain

1999

Admittance of Nunavut to
Canada as its third and
final territory

Official Name: Canada

Flag of Canada: At the flag's left and right edges are two wide, red vertical stripes. Between them is a white square. A red maple leaf stands in the center of the square. Maple leaves are a symbol of the country. The colors red and white come from Canada's history with France and England. Canada adopted the flag in 1965.

Area: 3,855,103 square miles (9,984,670 square kilometers)

Capital City: Ottawa

Important Cities: Toronto, Vancouver, Montreal

Population: 35,362,905 (July 2016)

WHERE PEOPLE LIVE

COUNTRYSIDE 18.2%

CITY 81.8%

JOBS

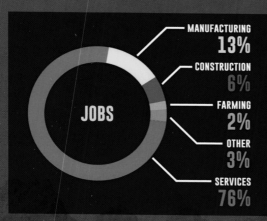

- MANUFACTURING **13%**
- CONSTRUCTION **6%**
- FARMING **2%**
- OTHER **3%**
- SERVICES **76%**

Main Exports:

oil

aircraft

chemicals

precious metals

forest products

cars and car parts

National Holiday:
Canada Day (July 1)

Main Languages:
English, French

Form of Government:
constitutional monarchy

Title for Country Leaders:
prime minister (head of government),
queen (head of state)

RELIGION

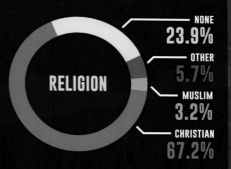

- NONE **23.9%**
- OTHER **5.7%**
- MUSLIM **3.2%**
- CHRISTIAN **67.2%**

Unit of Money:
Canadian dollar; one hundred cents make up one dollar.

GLOSSARY

aboriginals—the people who have been in a region from the earliest time

ancestors—relatives who lived long ago

export—to sell to a different country

First Nations—people whose ancestors lived in Canada before European explorers arrived; there are more than 600 First Nations groups in Canada.

Great Lakes—large freshwater lakes on the border between Canada and the United States; the Great Lakes that Canada touches are Superior, Huron, Erie, and Ontario.

immigrants—people who move to a new country

landmark—an important structure or place

migrate—to travel from one place to another, often with the seasons

native—originally from the area or related to a group of people that began in the area

natural resources—materials in the earth that are taken out and used to make products or fuel

nuclear families—families that include only the parents and children

patron saint—a saint who is believed to look after a country or group of people

plains—large areas of flat land

province—an area within a country; provinces follow all the laws of the country and make some of their own laws.

reserves—areas of land controlled by First Nations people

service jobs—jobs that perform tasks for people or businesses

symbol—something that stands for something else

traditions—customs, ideas, or beliefs handed down from one generation to the next

tundra—frozen, treeless land; beneath the surface, tundra is permafrost, or land that is permanently frozen.

urban—related to the city and city life

TO LEARN MORE

AT THE LIBRARY

Herman, Gail. *Who Is Wayne Gretzky?* New York, N.Y.: Grosset & Dunlap, 2015.

MacLeod, Elizabeth. *Canada Year by Year*. Toronto, Ont.: Kids Can Press, 2016.

Stine, Megan. *Where Is Niagara Falls?* New York, N.Y.: Grosset & Dunlap, 2015.

ON THE WEB

Learning more about Canada is as easy as 1, 2, 3.

1. Go to www.factsurfer.com.

2. Enter "Canada" into the search box.

3. Click the "Surf" button and you will see a list of related web sites.

With factsurfer.com, finding more information is just a click away.

INDEX